very first things to know about
bears

written by Deborah Kovacs

illustrated by
Richard Cowdrey

WORKMAN PUBLISHING
NEW YORK

1 A bear is a mammal.

Mammals have fur or hair.

Most female mammals give birth to live young and the babies feed on their mother's milk.

Baby bears are called cubs.

Squirrels and mice are mammals, too. Find a squirrel and a mouse on the sticker page. Put them in the picture.

2 **A bear has a big head with small eyes and round ears.**

Actual-size adult male Kodiak bear's canine tooth.

You have canine teeth, too. Open your mouth and look in a mirror to find your canine teeth.

A bear has a keen sense of hearing.

Bears have an excellent sense of smell.

Most bears have 42 teeth. Some teeth are sharp and pointed, for biting. They are called canine teeth.

3 A bear has powerful front paws.

A bear has five toes and five sharp claws on each foot. The front paws can be dangerous weapons. Most of the time, however, bears use them to find food.

A bear may use its paws to turn over rocks and logs in order to find insects.

A bear uses its front paws to rake berries from bushes and to dig up the ground to find tasty roots to eat.

Bears also use their paws to catch small rodents that live underground.

How many mice can you find hidden in this picture?

4 Bears can stand upright.

Sometimes bears stand on their hind legs to get a better look at what's going on around them or to reach food on a high tree branch.

Bears, like people, are plantigrades. That means they walk with their feet flat on the ground.

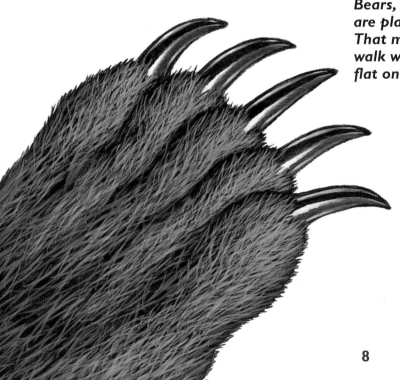

The bottoms of most bears' feet are naked. But polar bears have furry-bottomed feet. This helps to keep them from slipping on ice.

Find the sticker of the furry bottom of a polar bear's foot. Place it here.

Can you walk on all fours like a roly-poly bear?

Bears' two front feet turn inward when they walk.

A bear's hind footprints are similar to a person's footprints.

5 There are many different kinds of bears.

Different kinds of bears live in different places all around the world.

Sun bears are the smallest of all bears. They live in Southeast Asia.

Brown bears, which include grizzly and Kodiak bears, live in North America. A small number of brown bears also live in Europe.

Polar bears live in the Arctic.

Spectacled bears are the only bears that live in South America.

How many bears on these two pages have all white fur? How many have black-and-white fur? How many bears do you see altogether?

Sloth bears live in the forests of India, Nepal, and Sri Lanka.

Giant panda bears live in China.

Asian black bears, also called moon bears, live in the mountain forests of southern Asia.

American black bears live in North America.

6 Bears have enormous appetites.

Bears spend a lot of time looking for food. Bears eat different kinds of food depending on where they live, what time of year it is, and what they happen to find.

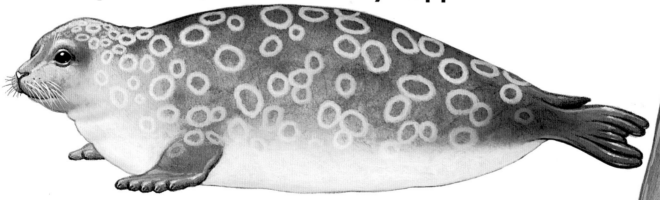

Most bears eat more plants than meat, except for the polar bear. Few plants grow in the cold Arctic, so the polar bear's favorite food is seals.

Some bears like to eat bugs. Find the stickers of bugs and put them on this page.

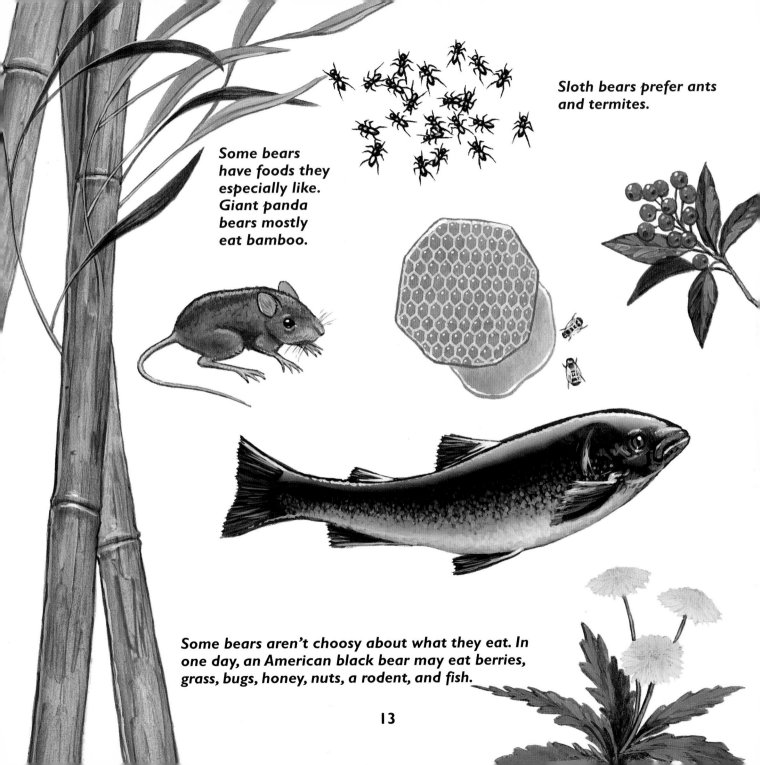

Sloth bears prefer ants and termites.

Some bears have foods they especially like. Giant panda bears mostly eat bamboo.

Some bears aren't choosy about what they eat. In one day, an American black bear may eat berries, grass, bugs, honey, nuts, a rodent, and fish.

13

7 Some bears are good at catching fish.

Brown bears return again and again to rivers they know will be full of salmon at certain times of the year.

Cubs learn to fish by watching their mother.

Sometimes a bear will stand on shore and pin down a fish with its paws. Bears also wade into the water to snag a fish between their teeth or dive right in to catch a fish underwater.

Find the four fish on the sticker page. Put them in the river for the bears to catch.

When salmon are plentiful, bears eat only the skin and eggs, which are the most nutritious parts of the fish.

8 Bears are smart, curious, and have good memories.

To prevent other animals from following them, bears have been known to cover their tracks by sweeping over their pawprints with leaves or branches.

start here

Find the pawprint stickers on the sticker page. Use them to show the path the brown bear took through the forest to reach the blueberry bushes.

Some bears will travel a long way to return to a place where they remember having found something tasty to eat—even if they have not been there for several years.

9 Bears have long, strong bodies.

Bears have short legs, which make them look slow and clumsy when they move, but they are among the strongest and fastest animals on earth. Most bears can run faster than people can.

Many kinds of bears are good swimmers, but polar bears are the best swimmers of all. They use their powerful front legs and huge webbed paws to propel themselves through the water. Polar bears can remain in icy waters for hours at a time.

Some bears are good tree climbers. Almost all bears like honey, but sun bears like honey so much they are sometimes called honey bears. Sun bears are particularly good at climbing trees. Perhaps that's because they're hoping to find a beehive in the branches.

Find the sticker of the beehive. Place it in the tree where the sun bear can find it.

10 A bear will defend its territory.

Each spring, an adult grizzly bear marks its territory, or the area where it lives. It rubs its body against trees so other bears can smell its scent.
It also makes "bear trees" by biting out large pieces of a tree's bark, and making slash marks on the trunk.

If another bear comes into a grizzly's territory, the grizzly might grunt, roar, or sometimes stand on its hind legs, trying to get the other bear to go away.

Why do you think the grizzly bear is standing on its hind legs and growling? Can you find the "bear tree" in this picture?

 # Some bears build dens where they stay during cold winter months.

Grizzly bears build dens where they stay for much of the winter. A den can be in a cave, a hollow tree, or a brush pile. It may even be a big, deep hole in the ground.

Using the number stickers on the sticker page, put the pictures in the order that tells the story of a bear getting ready for winter.

The bear curls up and goes to sleep.

The bear makes a bed using grass, leaves, and twigs.

Bears sleep for much of the winter. During its winter sleep, a bear does not eat or drink. It lives off the fat of its own body. Some bears sleep sitting up; others burrow down in their bedding and sleep curled up.

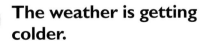 The weather is getting colder.

A grizzly bear looks for a place to stay for the winter.

12 Most bear cubs are born in the winter.

At certain times of the year, usually in spring, adult male and female bears mate. The following winter, the female bear will wake up from her long sleep to give birth to between one and four cubs.

Find the sticker of the newborn bear cub. Put it with its brother and its mother in the den.

A bear cub is tiny and helpless when it is born. It has almost no fur, and is blind. After the cub is born, its mother licks it clean, shows it how to nurse, and then goes back to sleep.

13 Cubs spend most of their day playing.

In spring, the mother bear and her cubs leave their den. The cubs spend their time playing and practicing the skills they will need as adults. By the time the cubs are two years old, they are ready to live on their own and find food for themselves.

Cubs may push one another down, chew each others' ears, or just growl, howl, and whine. They may also dig holes, fight over food, play hide-and-seek, or wrestle each other to the ground.

As the cubs play, their mother is always close by, keeping an eye on the little ones.

Find a sticker of a third bear cub. Have the cub climb on the tree stump or play with the other cubs.

14 For much of its life, a bear eats, sleeps, and travels alone.

Unless it's a mother bear with cubs, an adult bear lives alone almost all the time. No one knows why bears choose to live alone. Maybe it's because a bear on its own has a better chance of finding enough food to eat. In places where food is plentiful, several bears may gather together, but they will usually ignore each other.

Although there is only one bear in this picture, there are many other animals. How many animals can you find?

Most bears, left undisturbed, live between twenty and thirty years.

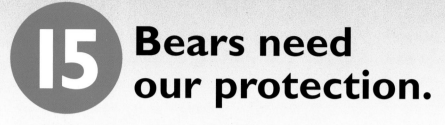

15 Bears need our protection.

Bears are big animals and they need a lot of room to roam. Mother bears need a safe place to raise their cubs.

Add some stickers of wildflowers, butterflies, and a bird to finish the picture of this wild, open place.

Bears need to live in areas where they won't come in contact with people, farms, or live-stock. By setting aside large areas of land, people try to leave enough wild, open places where bears can live in peace and freedom.

Answers

Pages 6–7: There are three mice in the picture.

Pages 10–11: One bear has all white fur. One bear has black-and-white fur. There are eight bears altogether.

Pages 20–21: The grizzly bear is standing on its hind legs and growling because another bear has come into its territory.

Pages 22–23: The order of the story is:

1. The weather is getting colder.
2. A grizzly bear looks for a place to stay for the winter.
3. The bear makes a bed using grass, leaves, and twigs.
4. The bear curls up and goes to sleep.

Pages 28–29: There are two birds, one squirrel, one rabbit, one raccoon, and one snake in the picture.

Published by
Workman Publishing Company, Inc.
708 Broadway
New York, NY 10003-9555

Printed in Spain

10 9 8 7 6 5 4 3 2 1

Library of Congress Cataloging-in-Publication Data

Kovacs, Deborah.
    Very first things to know about bears / by Deborah Kovacs; illustrated by Richard Cowdrey.
      p.   cm.
    ISBN 0-7611-0854-8
    1. Bears—Juvenile literature. 2. Toy and movable books—Specimens. [1. Bears. 2. Toy and movable books.]
    I. Cowdrey, Richard, ill. II. Title.
    QL737.C27K68 1997
    599.78—dc21   97-1648
                                                                                    CIP
                                                                                    AC

Designed by Nancy Loggins Gonzalez
With special thanks to Eric M. Brothers, Department of Mammalogy, AMNH